MISSION
ROME

Author: Catherine Aragon
Designer: Nada Orlić

CONTENTS

AFTER COMPLETING EACH MISSION, CHECK (√) THE BOX AND WRITE THE NUMBER OF POINTS EARNED.

AT THE END, WRITE THE TOTAL NUMBER OF POINTS HERE:

ATTENTION: FUTURE SPECIAL AGENTS ~~YOU~~

AND CASE OFFICERS ~~GROWNUPS~~

CONGRATULATIONS! THE SIA (SECRET INTERNATIONAL AGENCY) HAS SELECTED YOU AS A CANDIDATE TO BECOME A SPECIAL AGENT.

The SIA carries out important assignments, secretly collecting intelligence in all corners of the globe. ("Intelligence" is spy-speak for "information.") Currently, we are in dire need of agents. Many want to join us, but only a few have what it takes.

HOW WILL YOU PROVE YOU'RE READY TO JOIN THE MOST ELITE SPY AGENCY IN THE WORLD? You must complete a series of missions in Rome, Italy. Similar to a scavenger hunt (only better), these missions will require you to carry out challenging investigations and collect valuable intel (short for "intelligence"). For each mission, you'll earn points towards becoming a special agent.

YOUR ASSIGNMENT: TRAVEL TO ROME WITH YOUR TEAM, LED BY YOUR CASE OFFICER. (A case officer accompanies agents on missions. Your case officer is your parent or other trusted adult.) You must earn at least 100 points to become a SIA special agent.

-The mission list and mission scorecard are on page 1.

-Read the "Anytime Missions" early, so that you'll remain on alert and ready to earn points.

-You don't need to complete all of the missions to reach 100 points or complete them in any particular order.

BONUS MISSION

"Get Your Bonus Mission Today!"

Want even more Rome fun? Visit **Scavengerhuntadventures.Com/bonus** (all lowercase) today to download your **free bonus mission: "Rome's Obelisks."**

(Plus, you'll get *The Museum Spy*, our free e-book!)

MISSION RULES

- Be kind and respectful to team members.

- Your case officer (your parent or other trusted adult) has the final decision regarding point awards.

- Your case officer serves as the official "scorekeeper."

- Your case officer has the final decision on what missions will be attempted. (Don't worry, you can still earn enough points to become an agent without completing all the missions.)

- Always be on alert. You never know when a chance to earn points lies just around the corner.

TO CONCEAL THEIR REAL IDENTITIES, SPECIAL AGENTS ALWAYS USE CODE NAMES. FOR EXAMPLE, JAMES BOND'S CODE NAME IS 007. THINK OF YOUR OWN CODE NAME TO USE DURING YOUR MISSION IN ROME.

SIGN YOUR CODE NAME HERE:

....

_____

DATE

Important: For the missions you will need a pen or pencil and a camera. **LET THE MISSIONS BEGIN – GOOD LUCK!**

PRE-ARRIVAL BRIEF

AGENTS MUST HAVE SHARP SKILLS WHEN IT COMES TO ANALYZING IMAGES, SUCH AS PHOTOS, IN ORDER TO GATHER IMPORTANT INTEL.

"Intel" is short for "intelligence." Aerial photos like this one are taken from high in the sky by a satellite, a machine that orbits the Earth and takes pictures. Governments sometimes use satellites for spying, and other times simply for gathering information.

A satellite snapped this photo of Europe at night. The clusters of white light are night-time city lights.

Look at the outlines of Italy using the map, and then try to make out Italy in the satellite photo. Next, look at the location of Rome on the map. Then...

☑ **FIND ROME ON THE SATELLITE PHOTO AND CIRCLE IT.** (Remember, large cities like Rome will have the most lights.)

1 POINT

ROMAN FORUM

Rome's First Emperor: Augustus Caesar

Reg.I   FORO ROMANO   RX

The Forum was Ancient Rome's "downtown," the heart of the entire Roman Empire. Romans packed the streets of the Forum, on their way to shop at the busy markets, attend meetings at the Senate, worship at a grand temple, or visit a friend in a fancy palace.

25

- UMBILICUS URBIS
- MILLIARIUM AUREUM
- ARCH OF SEPTIMIUS SEVERUS
- COLUMN OF PHOCAS

- TEMPLES: CASTOR AND POLLUX, VESTA, ANTONINUS PIUS AND FAUSTINA, JULIUS CAESAR
- ARCH OF TITUS

TOTAL POINTS

Roman Forum in Ancient Times

SPECIAL AGENTS MUST HAVE A KEEN EYE FOR DETAIL. AGENTS ALWAYS NEED TO HAVE THEIR EYES PEELED FOR THE TINIEST CLUES – CRITICAL INFORMATION THAT OTHERS OFTEN MISS. IT'S TIME TO PUT YOUR SKILLS TO THE TEST.

☑ LOCATE THE UMBILICUS URBIS.

2 *POINTS*

Translated from Latin (the language of Ancient Rome) to English as "belly button," this plaque (near the Arch of Septimius Severus) marks what was once the center of the city. The Latin alphabet didn't have the letter "U," so look for the letters "Vmbilicvs Vrbis."

EUROPE

Atlantic Ocean

Rome

Mediterranean Sea

MIDDLE
EAST

AFRICA

Roman Empire at its peak

☑ HUNT DOWN THE MILLIARIUM AUREUM. **2** POINTS

Known as the "Golden Milestone," all of the roads
of the vast Roman Empire started from this marker,
located near the Umbilicus Urbis and the Temple of
Saturn. At its peak the empire was huge, stretching
all the way from present-day Portugal, Britain, Egypt,
and Iran. The empire's network of roads covered around
75,000 miles (121,000 km).

☑ **TRACK DOWN THE ARCH OF SEPTIMIUS SEVERUS.** `2 POINTS`

Roman emperors loved to construct grand arches
at prime spots throughout the city. They wanted
passers-by, like you, to gaze up at the towering
arch and remember Rome's impressive military
victories. This arch was built to honor the emperor
Severus and his sons Geta and Caracalla, after their
victory in Parthia, a region that is today Iran.

☑ **FIND THE PARTHIA BATTLE SCENES.** `1 POINT`

Although many of the heads in
the battle scene sculpture
were cut off, can you still
make out the soldiers'
helmets and shields?

☑ **LOCATE "VICTORIA."** `1 POINT`

The Roman goddess for
victory, "Victoria," appears
to honor Severus, Geta, and
Caracalla following their
triumph.

THE MOST CRITICAL PART OF A SPECIAL AGENT'S JOB IS COLLECTING INTELLIGENCE. INTELLIGENCE COMES IN MANY FORMS, INCLUDING PHOTOS. HUNT AROUND FOR THE NEXT THREE MONUMENTS, SNAPPING A PHOTO OF EACH.

☑ COLUMN OF PHOCAS **2** *POINTS*

Named in honor of the emperor Phocas, this tall column was constructed in 608. By this time, the original Roman Empire, which lasted for around 500 years (from 27 B.C. to 476), had split in two. The glory days for the Forum were long gone, and "New Rome," a city called "Constantinople" (nowadays, Istanbul, Turkey) replaced Rome as the new empire's center.

☑ TEMPLE OF CASTOR AND POLLUX *POINTS*

Although the twin brothers Castor and Pollux were originally Greek gods, the two miraculously appeared to help the Roman army win important battles, so the Romans constructed this temple as a grand "thank you" gift. When Castor died, Pollux (who was immortal) missed his brother, so the twins' father Zeus worked his magic and let the two split their time between life in the sky as gods and life as mortals (underground in Hades).

Today   Ancient Times

☑ **TEMPLE OF VESTA** **2 POINTS**

Here "vestals" kept Rome's
eternal flame burning bright.
Romans believed that as long
as the fire burned, Rome would
remain strong. Vestals were
priestesses (female priests)
carefully selected between
the ages of 6 and 10 to serve
Rome for a period of 30 years.
The young girls had to leave
their families behind, live in
a temple, and not marry until the 30 years was
up. Romans thought very highly of the vestals,
whom they believed had magical powers. Not only
were they trusted with Rome's eternal flame, they
even had their own ring-side VIP seats at the
Colosseum, quite an honor indeed.

my notes:

_____

_____

_____

Today

Ancient Times

☐ **TRACK DOWN THE REMAINS OF THE TEMPLE OF JULIUS CAESAR.**

The Roman people were so fond of Julius Caesar that they actually named a month, July, after him. However, not all Romans felt the same way. After Caesar was crowned "dictator-for-life" (in the year 44 B.C.), some grew quite suspicious of his power and soon **devised a plan to assassinate him.**

Caesar knew something was in the works, so **he recruited spies to collect information about the plot.** His agents worked swiftly and discovered that Caesar's own senators were behind the plan. Unfortunately for Caesar, the agents didn't know when the senators planned to act.

To uncover the date that the senators assassinated him, you must use a "Caesar Cipher" to decode the date on the next page. Before becoming a dictator, Caesar led Rome's army as a brave general. **To pass along top-secret military messages, he wrote them in secret code (using a "Caesar Cipher").** Each letter was encoded with a shift of three letters down the alphabet. For example, the code "dfh" is really the word "ace." (You move back three letters to break the code.)

A	B	C	D	E	F	G	H	I	J	K	L	M	N	O	P	Q	R	S	T	U	V	W	X	Y	Z
X	Y	Z	A	B	C	D	E	F	G	H	I	J	K	L	M	N	O	P	Q	R	S	T	U	V	W

Date of assassination:
Pdufk Iliwhhqwk

☑ DATE OF ASSASSINATION: **1** *POINT*
<u>March 15</u> 44, B.C.

Julius Caesar

Today

Ancient Times

☐ **LOCATE THE TEMPLE OF ANTONINUS PIUS** **2** *POINTS*
AND FAUSTINA.

Emperor Antoninus Pius loved his dear wife Faustina
so much that he built a temple in her memory and had
coins minted in her honor. (When Antoninus Pius died,
the Romans changed the name of this temple to honor
him, too.)

my notes:

....

....

Antoninus Pius

"Diva" Faustina's Coin

Centuries ago, during the Middle Ages, people tore down much of the Forum. They didn't care about the history behind these important sites – it was "out with the old and in with the new." They cut down towering columns as if they were trees, hauled them away, and hoisted them up again in a new palace or church (or they would tear apart the columns for their valuable stone).

☑ ANALYZE THE TEMPLE'S COLUMNS AND FIND THE CUT MARKS.

1 POINT

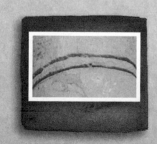

(People cut these deep into the stone, in the hope that the columns would fall over.)

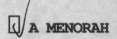 **FIND THE ARCH OF TITUS.** **2** *POINTS*

The emperor Domitian built this arch to celebrate the victory of his brother Titus in Israel in the year 71. Examine the arch and locate:

 A MENORAH **2** *POINTS*

A menorah resembles a candleholder and symbolizes Israel in the arch.

 TITUS **1** *POINT*

Following his victory, Titus rides away proudly in a horse-drawn carriage. (Through the centuries the horses have lost some legs.)

CAPITOLINE HILL

The Temple of Jupiter, honoring the King of the Gods, once stood atop Capitoline Hill with an excellent view over the Forum below. Today, Rome's city hall and Capitoline Museums stand watch over the Forum.

Outside the museums

☑ **FIND THE BRONZE STATUE OF EMPEROR MARCUS AURELIUS.**

Marcus Aurelius sits proudly atop his horse, with his right hand raised. He ruled from 161 to 180 and did such a good job that he made it on to the exclusive "Five Good Emperors" list created to size up Rome's rulers.

3

TOTAL POINTS

☐ **LOCATE THE STATUE OF ROMA.**

1 POINT

In Italian "Rome" = "Roma." It's also the name of the goddess of the city. She wears a dark purple dress.

☐ **TRACK DOWN THE STATUE OF TIBER, THE GOD WITH THE SAME NAME AS ROME'S RIVER.**

1 POINT

Tiber lounges, while Romulus and Remus play by his elbow. (See the story of Romulus and Remus on page 18.)

my notes:

_____

_____

CAPITOLINE MUSEUMS

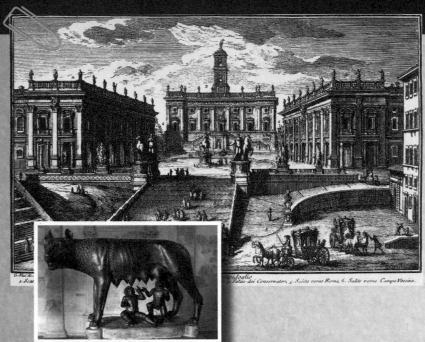

☐ FIND THE "CAPITOLINE WOLF," THE STATUE OF
THE SHE-WOLF NURSING TWO BABIES.

1 POINT

According to legend, the two babies are **Romulus and Remus,** sons of the god of war, Mars. The twins were abandoned at birth at the banks of Rome's Tiber River. The she-wolf rescued them, nursing them until a shepherd and his wife took the infants in as their sons. **The twins grew up and founded a new settlement (what would become Rome) in 753 B.C.** The twins got into a horrible fight over who would rule this new village. Romulus ended up killing Remus and named the village after himself.

9

TOTAL POINTS

☐ **LOCATE "MEDUSA," DISTURBED BY HER CRAZY HEAD OF SNAKES.**

1 POINT

☐ **TRACK DOWN THE BUST OF THE EMPEROR COMMODUS.**

1 POINT

Commodus loved to wrap animal skins (like this lion skin) around himself and pretend to be the god Hercules. **Commodus, the son of Emperor Marcus Aurelius** (the emperor in the bronze statue), **would rank high on a list of Rome's worst emperors.** Nothing was more important to Commodus than... Commodus. He invented so many new names for himself that he eventually had 12 names. He renamed the 12 months of the year using his 12 names. He even renamed Rome as the Colony of Commodus. It comes as no surprise that Commodus was assassinated (but it took three tries). Thankfully Rome's name was restored and the city removed almost all of the reminders of crazy Commodus.

☐ **FIND THE ORIGINAL VERSION OF THE STATUE WHOSE REPLICA YOU UNCOVERED OUTSIDE: MARCUS AURELIUS.**

The statue doesn't look too shabby, considering it's been around since the year 175. Bronze statues of Roman emperors that old are few and far between. Many were melted down for their bronze and then "recycled" into coins. If statues were lucky enough to make it past the "recyclers," they probably weren't so lucky during medieval times, when Christians tore down ancient statues, mistaking the emperors for Pagan gods. However, the Christians mixed up Emperor Marcus Aurelius with Emperor Constantine (Rome's first Christian emperor) so he avoided the chopping block.

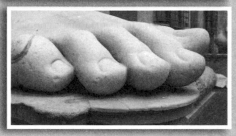

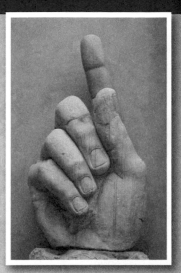

Speaking of Emperor Constantine, track down these remains from his colossal 40 feet tall (12 meters) statue, the *Colossus of Constantine*:

☐ **HEAD** **1** POINT

☐ **FOOT** **1** POINT

☐ **HAND** **1** POINT

Constantine's Coin

☐ STAND BESIDE CONSTANTINE'S HAND AND HAVE YOUR PHOTO TAKEN LOOKING UP TO THE CEILING AS IF YOU WANT TO SEE WHAT CONSTANTINE IS POINTING TOWARDS.

 2 POINTS

BOCCA DELLA VERITÀ

TOTAL POINTS

(Bocca della Verità = "Boka dellah Vare-ee-tah")

The mouth of this famous sculpture is the "Bocca della Verità" (the "Mouth of Truth" in English). This sculpture, located in the Church of Santa Maria in Cosmedin, serves as a sort of old-fashioned lie detector. Legend has it that if you've lied and you stick your hand in, then the mouth will bite it off.

Could you remove your hand from the mouth of truth…or would the mouth enjoy it as a snack? **Let's find out.**

☐ **HAVE YOUR PHOTO TAKEN PLACING YOUR HAND IN THE BOCCA DELLA VERITÀ.**

2 POINTS

(If the church gate is closed, then earn points by taking a photo of the sculpture.)

ARCH OF CONSTANTINE

Emperor Constantine ruled Rome about 1700 years ago as the empire's first Christian emperor. After beating his arch-rival Maxentius in an important battle, he proudly returned to the heart of the city, had a huge victory parade, and constructed this arch so that everyone would remember his triumph.

☑ **FIND THE SOLDIERS, ARMED WITH SHIELDS, SWORDS, AND HELMETS, FIGHTING AT THE CITY WALL.**

1 POINT

☐ **TRACK DOWN "SOL INVICTUS," THE SYMBOL OF THE SUN.**

1 POINT

The Sun rides in a chariot led by four horses. Emperor Constantine declared "Sunday," the day of the sun, as the Roman day of rest when businesses were closed and people got to relax.

COLOSSEUM

When ancient Romans wanted some entertainment (some very gory entertainment) they ventured to the Colosseum, an arena where thousands of gladiators and animals met their end. What you see today is less than half as large as the original arena which was "open for business" from 80 to around 520. Imagine yourself as an ancient Roman entering a stadium well over twice as large as today's, with a roaring crowd of over 50,000 spectators.

Back then the arena had a wooden floor, and the maze of stone passages you see today rested beneath. The gladiators (most of whom were criminals, slaves, or prisoners) and animals (such as lions, tigers, and bears) roamed this area before and after the "big event."

EMPEROR'S CROSS

VIP MARBLE SEATS

4

TOTAL POINTS

Where you sat depended on your social class. The "VIPs" (emperors, senators, and nobles) sat closest to the action in marble seats.

☑ **FIND THE CROSS MARKING THE EMPEROR'S BOX.**

2 POINTS

(This is where historians speculate the emperor had his VIP seat.)

☐ **FIND THE GROUP OF VIP MARBLE SEATS.**

2 POINTS

25

BASILICA SAN CLEMENTE

(Clemente = "Clay-men-tay")

San Clemente

SPECIAL AGENTS MUST ALWAYS REMAIN ON ALERT.

While inside this church, stay on alert and find
two things:

☐ **ANCHORS** **2** *POINTS*

These are the symbols of San Clemente (Saint Clement),
for whom the church is named. He was drowned in the
sea with an anchor around his neck.

☐ **THE SOUND OF RUSHING WATER** **2** *POINTS*

☐ **BONUS: BEFORE LEAVING, FOLLOW YOUR EARS** **3** *POINTS*
   AND TRACK DOWN THE SOURCE OF THE WATER.

- ANCHORS
- RUSHING WATER
- MOSAIC
- MITHRAS CHAMBER

TOTAL POINTS

Track down the mosaic of Christ upon the cross with the Tree of Life at the bottom. A "mosaic" is a picture made of small pieces of colored glass or colored stone.

☐ **FIND SAINT CLEMENT IN THE MOSAIC.**

2 POINTS

Hint: He holds an anchor and stands atop a boat.

Like other churches in Rome, this place was built atop the remains of an ancient temple. **Can you carry out the rest of this mission even though it requires you to descend into a spooky dungeon-like chamber used in ancient times by a mysterious cult?** After successfully passing unusual initiation ceremonies, members of the cult of Mithras greeted each other with secret handshakes and met in temples like this.

☐ **TRACK DOWN THE GOD OF MITHRAS, WEARING A FLOWING CAPE.**

2 POINTS

SPANISH STEPS

What makes the famous Spanish Steps "Spanish?"
Near the base of the steps, at #57 Piazza di
Spagna *("Pee-aht-zah Dee Spahg-nah")* (Spain
Plaza), stands Spain's embassy to the Vatican.

☑ **HUNT DOWN THE SPANISH EMBASSY, THE** **2** POINTS
NAMESAKE OF THE SPANISH STEPS.

(Hint: Look for the Spanish flag and the Virgin Mary standing
atop a large column.)

Through the ages Rome's river,
the Tiber, has given the city
its fair share of floods. One
of the worst on record occurred
in 1598. Rome's residents had
to navigate around the city
in boats. Once the flood water finally went away, an
abandoned boat remained in this plaza. As a reminder
of the flood, an Italian sculptor, Pietro Bernini
("Pee-etro Ber-nee-nee"), together with his son, Gian
Lorenzo *("Jahn Lorenzo")*, created the *Fountain of the
Old Boat.*

7

- SPANISH EMBASSY
- OLD BOAT FOUNTAIN
- THE STEPS

TOTAL POINTS

☑ **HAVE YOUR PHOTO TAKEN STANDING ON** **2** POINTS
THE BOAT'S "DOCK." (AND BE SURE NOT TO FALL
INTO THE WATER!)

Gian Lorenzo Bernini

You also need to verify some "intelligence."
According to some sources, you must climb 137
steps to the top. Other sources list 135 or 138.

☑ **CLIMB TO THE TOP OF THE SPANISH STEPS AND** **3** POINTS
COUNT THE NUMBER OF STEPS.

166

my notes:

29

TREVI FOUNTAIN

(Trevi = "Trev-ee")

Legend has it that if you throw a coin into the Trevi Fountain, you're destined to return to Rome someday. What do you think - fact or fiction? Can tossing a coin into the fountain determine your future?

It's worth a shot.

Organize your team with your backs to the fountain. Make sure everyone has a coin.

7

TOTAL POINTS

- COIN TOSS/PHOTO
- MARCUS AGRIPPA SCULPTURE
- TRITONS
- ACE OF CUPS

☑ **ON THE COUNT OF 3 (1-2-3) EVERYONE MUST THROW A COIN OVER THEIR SHOULDER AND INTO THE FOUNTAIN.** **2** *POINTS*

If there are too many people around the fountain to do this, then:

☑ **STAND WITH YOUR BACK TO THE FOUNTAIN AND AS YOU TOSS IN A COIN, HAVE YOUR PHOTO TAKEN.** **2** *POINTS*

Any idea how much money people throw into the fountain each day? Around 3000 euros (approximately 4100 U.S. dollars or 2500 British pounds). The money goes to charity, so the euros you just tossed in will go to a good cause.

my notes:

• An aqueduct built by Marcus Agrippa (the general whose name you have to find carved on the Pantheon) supplies the fountain's water, and this water completes quite a journey. First it travels over 8 miles (13km) from a spring outside Rome through the 2,000-year-old aqueduct. Then it gushes out of the Trevi sculptures, drains away from the fountain, and hurries on to fill other fountains in the city, like the Fountain of the Old Boat at the Spanish Steps (page 28) and the Fountain of the Four Rivers at Piazza Navona (page 40).

☑ **FIND THE ABOVE SCULPTURE OF MARCUS AGRIPPA APPROVING PLANS FOR THE AQUEDUCT'S CONSTRUCTION.**

2
POINTS

While the aqueduct may be 2,000 years old, the actual fountain was built less than 300 years ago, in the 1700's. At the center stands Neptune, ••• the God of Sea, pulled in a chariot by horses and tritons.

Tritons are part-man, part-animal and similar to a mermaid.

☐ **WHAT ANIMAL ARE THEY?**

1
POINT

Neptune

Ace of Cups

When the fountain was under construction, a barbershop sat just across the street. Every day, the barber would hassle the fountain's sculptor about his design. Finally, the sculptor had enough, so one night he placed a big sculpture at the fountain's edge to block the barber's view and quiet his pesky criticisms. The sculpture, called the "Ace of Cups" is the symbol shown on an ace card from an Italian card game.

☑ **HUNT DOWN THE ACE OF CUPS.** **POINTS**

Take a few steps back to stand in front of the building directly behind it. What do you think? Does this block your view of the fountain?

PANTHEON

Marcus Agrippa

Hadrian

Outside the temple

A Roman general, Marcus Agrippa, had built a temple on this site; however it burned to the ground in a devastating fire. Emperor Hadrian completed the temple you see today, but credited Marcus Agrippa with an inscription on the front.

☑ **FIND MARCUS AGRIPPA'S LAST NAME INSCRIBED IN LARGE LETTERS.**

2 POINTS

19

- AGRIPPA INSCRIPTION
- COLUMNS
- DRAIN HOLES
- NICHES
- TOMBS OF VICTOR EMMANUEL AND MARGHERITA
- PIAZZA DELLA MINERVA OBELISK AND FLOOD MARKERS

TOTAL POINTS

☑ HOW MANY COLUMNS STAND AT THE ENTRANCE?

Each one stands about 40 feet (12 meters) tall and weighs 60 tons. Imagine hauling these from a quarry around 2,500 miles (4,000km) away in Egypt. These were dragged on wooden sledges, floated by barge down the Nile River, transferred to vessels for crossing the Mediterranean Sea, unloaded at the nearby port of Ostia, and finally arrived in Rome via barge on the Tiber River.

☑ HAVE A TEAMMATE SNAP YOUR PICTURE ATTEMPTING TO SPREAD YOUR ARMS AROUND ONE OF THESE MIGHTY COLUMNS.

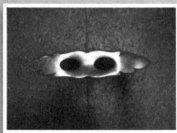

Inside the temple

Look up at the *oculus*, the temple's 27 foot (8 meter) wide "skylight." This is the Pantheon's only source of light. There's no glass over the oculus, so when it rains, raindrops fall into the Pantheon. However, the temple's smart architects designed the floor slightly curved and with tiny holes so the rainwater could drain out.

☐ UNCOVER A SET OF DRAIN HOLES. **2** POINTS

In between the columns inside lie "niches," one for each of the planetary gods worshipped by the Romans (Venus, Saturn, Mercury, and so on).

15

☑ HOW MANY NICHES ARE THERE? **2** POINTS

☑ **FIND THE TOMB FOR VICTOR EMMANUEL II, ITALY'S FIRST KING.**

Victor Emmanuel = Vittorio Emanuele ("Vee-tor-ee-oh Eh-man-yoo-ell-ay") in Italian. Check out his mustache! Before his rule in the late 1800's, Italy was separated into different states, each with its own rulers, and some parts even controlled by foreign countries. The tomb of Victor Emmanuel's son, King Umberto, rests here, as well as the tomb of Umberto's wife, Queen Margherita, for whom Italy named a famous pizza.

The toppings (basil, mozzarella, and tomato sauce) represent the colors of the Italian flag (green, white, and red).

☑ **FIND THE TOMB OF QUEEN MARGHERITA.**

☑ BONUS: WHILE IN ROME, TRY A MARGHERITA PIZZA.

1 POINT

NEAR THE PANTHEON

Around the corner from the Pantheon lies the Piazza della Minerva. (Standing outside of the Pantheon, face the temple and walk to the left, around the corner.) The piazza name comes from the church in the square, Santa Maria sopra Minerva. The church is named in honor of St. Mary (Santa Maria) as well as Minerva, the goddess of magic, medicine, and wisdom.

☑ **WHAT ANIMAL CARRIES AN OBELISK UPON ITS BACK?**

2 POINTS

In the 1600's, the obelisk was discovered buried deep underneath the church's garden. Considering it's about 2500 years old, the obelisk looks pretty good. Emperor Diocletian brought it here from Egypt around the year 300.

Track down the markers (like this one) showing the high-level marks of the city's floods through the centuries.

☑ **HAVE YOUR PHOTO TAKEN STANDING UNDER THE HIGHEST ONE.**

Imagine water at this height flooding Rome's streets. One of these marks the flood of 1598 when the water rose over 13 feet (four meters) above the present street level in some parts of the city.

PIAZZA NAVONA

(Piazza Navona = "Pee-aht-zah Nah-vone-ah")

AS YOU KNOW, HAVING A KEEN EYE FOR DETAILS IS A MUST FOR SPECIAL AGENTS. AGENTS FREQUENTLY HAVE TO ANALYZE PIECES OF INTELLIGENCE, SEARCHING FOR SMALL DETAILS THAT PROVIDE VALUABLE CLUES.

Piazza (not "pizza!") means plaza. Put your spy skills to the test by tracking down the Fountain of the Four Rivers, and find the statues representing four rivers of the world.

9

- FOUR STATUES OF THE FOUR RIVERS FOUNTAIN
- FOUR KINDS OF ANIMALS
- EMPEROR'S NAME

TOTAL POINTS

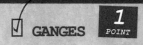

☑ **GANGES** **1** POINT

He holds a large oar, showing how easy it is to navigate this river which begins in India.

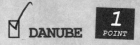

☑ **DANUBE** **1** POINT

He is about to touch a pope's crest. The Danube is the closest of the four rivers to the pope's residence.

☑ **NILE** **1** POINT

A cloth covers his head because back in the 1600's when this fountain was built, people didn't know where the Nile, a river in eastern Africa, had its source.

📖 **PLATA** `1 POINT`

The Plata River (the "Silver River," as in silver coins) flows through Argentina and Uruguay, which were once colonies of Spain. "Plata" sits atop a pile of coins, representing the riches that the colonies would bring to Europe.

Many kinds of animals creep and swim around in the fountains of Piazza Navona.

TRACK DOWN THESE ANIMALS:

☐ CROCODILE `1 POINT`

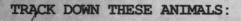

☑ DOLPHINS `1 POINT`
See photo above.

☒ HORSES `1 POINT`

☐ LION `1 POINT`

Almost 2,000 years ago on this site the Circus Agonalis opened its doors. Look closely and you can make out the shape of the stadium in the piazza. Thirty thousand Romans could pack into this arena to enjoy sporting events and gladiator fights.

The Emperor

The stadium was built by an emperor so cruel, **his own court officials hatched a plot to assassinate him.**

The emperor knew his days were numbered, so he sought the advice of an astrologer. The story goes that **the astrologer told him he would die by noon on September 18 of the year 96.** September 18 arrived. Hoping the hour of his death had passed, that morning the emperor asked a boy for the time. **The boy lied to the emperor,** stating it was past noon. Thinking he was clear, the emperor let his guard down and his killer struck. The killer, a servant, had faked an arm injury in order to sneak a dagger past palace guards.

The Romans wanted to forget that this emperor ever existed, so they destroyed his statues. However, not all reminders could be erased. Who was this emperor? **To find his name, hunt around for a street sign along the plaza's walls like this one.**

☑ DISCOVER THE EMPEROR'S NAME BELOW THE WORDS "PIAZZA NAVONA." HINT: HIS NAME CONTAINS THE LETTER "M."

1
POINT

PIAZZA R.VI
NAVONA

CASTEL SANT'ANGELO

According to the laws of Ancient Rome, the dead had to be buried outside the city. In ancient times, this castle lay just outside the city limits. Emperor Hadrian selected this prime site beside the Tiber River, as close to the city limits as possible, as the final resting place for himself and his family. Hadrian thought pretty highly of himself, so he designed it complete with a huge bronze statue of himself, as well as lush gardens and a grand temple. The years flew by and Hadrian bit the dust before the completion of his memorial site.

Not much remains of Hadrian's temple. The structure you see today has served as a prison, fortress, an "escape-of-last-resort" for the pope, and finally a museum.

☐ FIND THE MODEL OF HADRIAN'S TEMPLE.

- HADRIAN'S TEMPLE MODEL
- ANGEL MICHAEL STATUE
- POPE ALEXANDER'S CREST
- OLD WEAPONS
- VIEW FROM THE TOP

TOTAL POINTS

The castle is named in honor of the angel Michael (Castel Sant'Angelo = Castle of the Holy Angel). In the 500's, an awful disease spread through Italy and many nearby countries, killing thousands of people every day. According to legend, in the year 590, Michael landed atop the fortress and brought about an end to this horrible disease called the plague (unfortunately the plague came back in the 600's).

☐ **FIND THE STATUE OF THE ANGEL MICHAEL.**

2 POINTS

☐ **FIND THE CREST OF POPE ALEXANDER VI DECORATING THE CASTLE'S OLD WELL.**

2 POINTS

Pope Alexander VI is one of history's most notorious* popes. Through the years in plays, TV shows, and video games, Pope Alexander (also known as Rodrigo Borgia) plays the bad guy - the ring leader of a scandalous family, who takes bribes and gives the Catholic Church a bad name.

*notorious = famous for something bad

Pope Alexander VI

In order to defend fortresses, you must have
excellent views of approaching enemies as well as
high-tech weapons. Centuries ago, castle soldiers
would fight off enemies using these weapons. If
the enemies were "lucky" enough to find a way
past, soldiers would pour hot oil on them.

FIND:

☐ THE CATAPULT

1 POINT

☐ CANNONS

1 POINT

☐ PILES OF CANNONBALLS

1 POINT

Saint Peter's

Victor Emmanuel II

AGENTS MUST HAVE SHARP EYES TO SPOT THINGS FROM A DISTANCE. IN THE FIELD, SOMETIMES YOU CAN'T DEPEND ON ZOOM LENSES OR BINOCULARS FOR ASSISTANCE, JUST YOUR OWN TWO EYES.

SPOT THESE:

☐ SAINT PETER'S BASILICA

1 POINT

☐ VICTOR EMMANUEL II MONUMENT

1 POINT

☐ THE PANTHEON ROOF

☐ PASSETTO DI BORGO PASSAGE

In the 1200's, a secret passage was built to connect the fortress to the Vatican so that in times of war, the pope could safely escape to this mighty fortress. (It's not so secret anymore.)

Passetto di Borgo

Pantheon Roof

SAINT PETER'S BASILICA

Before you stands the most important church in the world. Believers from all corners of the globe venture here to see the pope, the leader of the Catholic Church. This, the world's largest church, could fit at least 60,000 people inside, and it rests inside the Vatican City, the smallest country in the world, measuring less than 0.2 square miles (0.5 square km) and home to around 850 people.

St. Peter's Square

The Swiss Guard (so called because their members come from Switzerland) protects the Vatican.

☑ **TRACK DOWN A MEMBER OF THE GUARD AND SNAP HIS PHOTO.**

2 POINTS

31

- SWISS GUARD MEMBER
- VATICAN STAMPS
- COMPASS
- HOLY DOOR
- DOVES, VATICAN CRESTS

- "PETRUS"
- SAINT PETER'S STATUE
- PIETÀ
- HOLY DOOR'S OTHER SIDE
- DOME CLIMB
- VIEW FROM THE TOP

TOTAL POINTS

The tiny country has its own postal service, complete with Vatican stamps.

☑ **BUY VATICAN STAMPS AND USE THEM TO SEND A POSTCARD TO SOMEONE SPECIAL BACK HOME.**

2 POINTS

(Note: You can buy Vatican stamps near the tourist office in the square.)

SUPER BONUS:

If you can complete this clue, then you are truly meant to be a secret agent. Somewhere on Saint Peter's square lies this design of a compass.

☑ **HUNT DOWN THE COMPASS AND FIND THE MARKERS ON THE GROUND FOR NORTH ("NORD") AND SOUTH ("SUD").**

5 POINTS

(When there's a festival, some of the parts of the square may be blocked off.
If so, then earn points by spotting the compass from the view atop St. Peter's dome.)

Entrance Hall

Upon entering, you must stroll through a huge hallway with large white columns and a ceiling decorated with gold.

☑ **FIND THE "HOLY DOOR."** **2 POINTS**

Hint: Bronze doors stand in the entrance hall, and on the bottom row of the Holy Door you'll uncover an image of the pope holding a cross and a hammer.

Don't even try to open the "Holy Door." It's only opened every 25 years, during a Holy Year (called the "Jubilee"). The next one takes place in 2025. In a ceremony, pilgrims wait outside the door. Then the pope bangs a hammer, opens the door, and welcomes the pilgrims.

Inside the church

WHILE INSIDE, YOU MUST REMAIN ON ALERT AND LOCATE:

☑ **TEN VATICAN CRESTS** 2 POINTS

(represented by the pope's crown and two keys)

☑ **TEN DOVES** 2 POINTS

☑ **BONUS: UNCOVER THE DOVE IN THE STAINED GLASS WINDOW.** 2 POINTS

Saint Peter's is named after history's first pope. Saint Peter was a close friend of Jesus and attempted to spread Christianity in Rome, but Ancient Rome's leaders would have nothing of it. The story goes that they were going to kill him the same way Jesus had died, on the cross. However, Peter demanded that he be placed upside down upon the cross. He felt that he was not worthy of dying the exact same way Jesus died. This church is built upon Peter's grave.

Saint Peter

LOCATE THE NEXT TWO REMINDERS OF SAINT PETER:

☑ "PETRUS" ABOVE THE ALTAR IN HUGE BLUE LETTERS ON A GOLD BACKGROUND

2 POINTS

"Petrus" is Latin for Peter. (The Latin alphabet uses a "v" instead of a "u," so Petrus will look like "Petrvs.")

☑ A BRONZE STATUE OF SAINT PETER

2 POINTS

His toes have been polished to a shine by people touching them for good luck.

☑ TRACK DOWN THE SCULPTURE PIETÀ.

2 POINTS

"Pietà" ("*Pee-eh-tah*") means "pity" in Italian. This sculpture shows Mary, the mother of Jesus, filled with pity and sorrow, holding Jesus in her lap following his death upon the cross. The Italian artist Michelangelo (*"Mee-kel-an-jelo"*) sculpted this famous work. Many sculptors sign their sculptures, but Michelangelo didn't sign his, except for this one. Closely examine Mary.

☑ BONUS: FIND THE RIBBON WITH WRITING CARVED ON IT (IT CONTAINS HIS NAME).

1 POINT

Castel Sant' Angelo

Passetto Di Borgo

☐ **FIND THE OTHER SIDE OF THE HOLY DOOR.**   **1** *POINT*

Remember the Holy Door you found? This is the other side - decorated with a gold cross and sealed with concrete (to make sure it stays shut for 25 years).

The Dome

SPECIAL AGENTS MUST BE IN TOP-NOTCH SHAPE. THIS MISSION WILL TEST YOUR PHYSICAL STRENGTH — GET READY FOR A HIKE!

☐ **CLIMB THE 550 STEPS TO THE TOP OF SAINT PETER'S FOR A BIRD'S-EYE VIEW OF THE CITY.**

(Or if you want to save your energy, then take the elevator to cut down on your climbing time.)

UNCOVER THESE LANDMARKS (SEE THE PHOTOS ABOVE):

☐ **TIBER RIVER**   **1** *POINT*

☐ **CASTEL SANT'ANGELO**   **1** *POINT*

☐ **PASSETTO DI BORGO PASSAGE**   **1** *POINT*

In the 13th century, this secret passage was built connecting the Vatican to the Castel Sant'Angelo so that in times of war, the pope could flee to the Castel Sant'Angelo. (It's not so secret anymore.)

SISTINE CHAPEL

The Ceiling

The ceiling of this famous chapel is covered with scenes from the Bible. The Italian artist Michelangelo (*"Mee-kel-an-jelo"*) painted the ceiling by hand (with a little help from his assistants). Look up at the ceiling soaring 70 feet (21 meters) above ground. Michelangelo had to create a special scaffold to support himself during the long four years (1508–1512) that it took to finish the ceiling. Imagine having to lie on your back painting for that long!

FIND GOD CREATING:

☑ **MAN**

2 POINTS

(symbolized by God, the one with the beard, reaching out his strong hand to touch the hand of Adam)

☑ **WOMAN**

2 POINTS

(symbolized by a woman, Eve, kneeling near God)

☑ **THE SUN AND MOON**

2 POINTS

(Correction: there are **two** moons!)

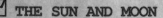

10

- GOD CREATES MAN, WOMAN, THE SUN AND MOON

- THE DEVIL SERPENT

- SELF-PORTRAIT IN THE LAST JUDGMENT

TOTAL POINTS

The evil devil finds his way into the painting too, in the form of a half snake-half human creature twisting around a tree.

☑ **LOCATE THE DEVIL.** **2** POINTS

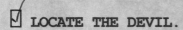
The Last Judgment

In this painting, Christ has returned for the final judgment of all mankind. There's chaos as everyone is destined for either heaven (the top of the painting) or hell (the bottom of the painting).

Michelangelo painted himself in this piece, with elements showing his own face (brown hair, brown eyes) in a horrible human-like image resembling a Halloween costume that hangs from a man's hand.

☑ **FIND MICHELANGELO'S SCARY SELF-PORTRAIT.** **2** POINTS

Michelangelo

ANYTIME MISSIONS

THE BEST AGENTS HAVE A HIGH LEVEL OF SOMETHING CALLED "SITUATIONAL AWARENESS." THESE QUICK-WITTED AGENTS PAY CLOSE ATTENTION TO THEIR SURROUNDINGS — READY TO COLLECT CRITICAL INTELLIGENCE AND RESPOND TO DANGEROUS SITUATIONS. HAVING EXCELLENT "SITUATIONAL AWARENESS" (SA FOR SHORT) MEANS ALWAYS BEING "ON ALERT."

These missions will test your SA. You can complete these at any time during your stay. Don't let your guard down as you wander around Rome, or you may miss a chance to win points.

ITALIAN FOOD: **FOUR POINTS MAX FOR THIS PART.**

To properly blend in, you'll need to eat Italian food. In a foreign country nothing blows your cover more than eating only hamburgers and French fries. Besides, don't you want to tell your friends back home about all the authentic pizza you ate in Italy, the country that invented it?

☐ HUNT DOWN THE MOST UNUSUAL PIZZA TOPPING YOU CAN FIND.

☐ TRY THIS UNUSUAL TOPPING ON YOUR NEXT SLICE OF PIZZA.
   (Don't worry, you can pick it off if it doesn't suit your taste.)

Now, the same for gelato (*"jeh-lah-toe"*).

☐ **HUNT DOWN THE MOST UNUSUAL GELATO FLAVOR YOU CAN FIND.** **1** POINT

☐ **TRY A SMALL SAMPLE OF THIS FLAVOR.** **1** POINT

SPEAKING ITALIAN: **THREE POINTS MAX FOR THIS PART.**

Time to put your language skills to the test! Below you'll find some situations to test your Italian.

Earn one point each time you say one of these Italian phrases to a different Italian person.

☐ **SAY "HELLO"** (for example to the staff at your hotel) **"BUON GIORNO"** (*Bwohn-jor-no*) **1** POINT

☐ **SAY "THANK YOU"** (for example after someone has just served you pizza or gelato) **"GRAZIE"** (*Graht-zee*) **1** POINT

☐ **SAY "GOODBYE"** (for example to the staff at your hotel) **"ARRIVEDERCI"** (*Ah-ree-vay-der-chee*) **1** POINT

NASONI

Public drinking fountains called "nasoni" (*"nah-so-nee"*) dot the city of Rome (around 2500 in total). The water is safe to drink, but the trick is to figure out how to do so without getting wet.

☐ **ONE POINT FOR EACH "NASONI" YOU SPOT (5 POINTS MAX)**
1 POINT

☐ **TWO POINTS FOR DRINKING FROM A "NASONI"**
2 POINTS

SPQR

Rome's official symbol, the initials "SPQR," comes from the Latin phrase "Senatus Populusque Romanus," meaning "The Senate and People of Rome." Remember, the ancient Romans spoke Latin. This saying summed up the belief that the Roman people (and not a king) controlled Roman society. SPQR appears on things like flags, arches, fountains, and manhole covers.

☐ **ONE POINT FOR EACH 'SPQR' YOU FIND (7 POINTS MAX)**
1 POINT

(To receive each point, the SPQR must be on a different kind of item. For example, once you have found 'SPQR' on a manhole cover, then that's all the points for "SPQR" on manhole covers.)

Anytime Missions: Bonus

COME ACROSS A MONUMENT OR EXHIBIT THAT'S CLOSED? NOT ENOUGH TIME IN ROME? HAVE NO FEAR, USE THESE MISSIONS TO ACHIEVE YOUR GOAL. YOUR CASE OFFICER SETS THE POINTS.

ITALIAN EUROS

Italy's currency is the euro, a currency shared among approximately 18 other European nations. Countries have their own national symbols imprinted on the coins. Track down a 5-cent Italian Euro coin.

☐ **WHAT ROMAN MONUMENT APPEARS ON THE BACK?**

Locate a 50-cent Italian Euro coin.

☐ **WHAT ROMAN EMPEROR APPEARS ON THE BACK?**

Hint: His statue stands atop Capitoline Hill.

ROME SOCCER

☐ **TRACK DOWN A JERSEY FOR A.S. ROMA, ONE OF THE CITY'S SOCCER TEAMS.**

Sold in many souvenir shops, these jerseys feature the team colors of burgundy and yellow and usually show the team's emblem.

☐ **WHAT SYMBOL OF ROME IS ON THE EMBLEM?**

ANSWER KEY

Once an answer is submitted, your case officer can check it here. If you peek at this answer key before submitting a final answer, you won't receive any points for that clue. Most clues do not have one correct answer, for those that do, here are the answers.

-Rome soccer: The Capitoline Wolf (with Romulus and Remus) appears on the emblem.

#15 Anytime Missions:
-Italian coins: The Colosseum appears on the back of a 5-cent coin. Marcus Aurelius appears on the back of a 50-cent coin.

#11 Piazza Navona: The emperor's name: Domiziano (in Italian, on the sign); Domitian (English translation).
-An elephant carries an obelisk upon its back.
-There are 7 niches.
-There are 16 columns.

#10 Pantheon:

#9 Trevi Fountain: Tritons are half-fish.

#8 Spanish Steps: The number of steps: the number YOU count!

#1 Roman Forum: Caesar died on March Fifteenth, 44 B.C.

#A Pre-Arrival Brief: See photo.

Note: the information in this book was accurate as of October 2013. We hope that you won't find anything outdated related to the clues. If you do find that something has changed, please email us at info@ScavengerHuntAdventures.com to kindly let us know.

We hope you enjoyed the missions. Comments or suggestions? We'd love to hear from you.

Contact us at info@ScavengerHuntAdventures.com.

THE FINAL MISSION

Case officers, please visit
scavengerhuntadventures.com/bonus
(all lowercase letters)

☐ **JOIN 'THE INSIDER' (OUR EMAIL LIST)**
You'll get a special bonus mission for
this city plus our free e-book,
The Museum Spy.

"I'm Joining
Today!"

PLEASE HELP SPREAD THE WORD

"We'd Love
To Help!"

We're a small family business and would be
thrilled if you **left a review online*** or
recommended our books to a friend.

Our books: Paris, London, Amsterdam, Rome, NYC, D.C.,
Barcelona, Florence, St. Augustine, with more coming!

*We can't mention the site name here, but it begins with "AM"!

A BIG THANK YOU

Photo by A1C Harry Brexel

Thank you for supporting
our family owned business.
Mom writes, Dad serves in the military, Grandma
is VP of Logistics and Jr. helps research
our books. **Without you this series wouldn't
be possible.**   Thank YOU!

Catherine

www.ScavengerHuntAdventures.com